Incredible Insects

John Townsend

Raintree

www.raintreepublishers.co.uk

Visit our website to find out more information about **Raintree** books.

To order:
☎ Phone 44 (0) 1865 888113
🖹 Send a fax to 44 (0) 1865 314091
🖥 Visit the Raintree Bookshop at **www.raintreepublishers.co.uk** to browse our catalogue and order online.

First published in Great Britain by Raintree, Halley Court, Jordan Hill, Oxford OX2 8EJ, part of Harcourt Education. Raintree is a registered trademark of Harcourt Education Ltd.

Editorial: Charlotte Guillain and Diyan Leake
Design: Michelle Lisseter and Kamae Design
Picture Research: Maria Joannou
Production: Jonathan Smith

Originated by Ambassador Litho Ltd
Printed and bound in Hong Kong, China by South China Printing Company

ISBN 1 844 43332 3
08 07 06 05 04
10 9 8 7 6 5 4 3 2 1

British Library Cataloguing in Publication Data
Townsend, John
Incredible Insects. – (Incredible Creatures)
595.7
A full catalogue record for this book is available from the British Library.

Acknowledgements

The publisher would like to thank the following for permission to reproduce photographs: Corbis pp. **6**, **19** top, **23** (Galen Rowell), **24** left (Bohemian Nomad Picturemakers), **34–35** (George D. Lepp), **50–51** (B. Borrell Casals/Frank Lane Picture Agency), **51** (Naashon Zalk); FLPA pp. **5** (top, middle, bottom), **7** left, **8**, **10**, **12** left, **13**, **14**, **16**, **17**, **22**, **22–23**, **24** right, **26–27**, **28–29**, **32–33**, **35**, **36**, **37**, **36–37**, **39** left, **39** right, **40–41**; Getty Images (Stone) p. **11** left; Natural Visions (Brian Rogers) p. **7** right; Naturepl pp. **4** (Bruce Davidson), **44** (Premaphotos); Nature Picture Library (Andrew Cooper) p. **9**; NHPA pp. **8–9**, **12** right, **15** left, **15** right, **16–17**, **18**, **19** bottom, **25**, **30**, **30–31**, **33**, **34**, **38**, **40**, **41**, **42–43**, **43**, **45**, **46**, **47**, **46–47**, **48**, **49**; Oxford Scientific Films pp. **11** right, **29**, **42**, **48–49**; Premaphotos Wildlife pp. **26** (Jean Preston-Mafham), **32** (Ken Preston Mafham); RSPCA Photolibrary p. **5** left; Science Photo Library pp. **20** top (Darwin Dale), **20** bottom, **21**, **27** (Dr Jeremy Burgess), **28** (Dr Jeremy Burgess), **31**, **44–45** (Darwin Dale/Agstock), **50**.

Cover photograph of a horsefly reproduced with permission of the RSPCA Photolibrary

The publishers would like to thank Jon Pearce for his assistance in the preparation of this book.

Contents

Any words appearing in the text in bold, **like this**, are explained in the Glossary. You can also look out for them in the 'Wild words' bank at the bottom of each page.

Incredible insects

Would you believe it?

- Many insects are so small you cannot see them. Some fairy flies are just 0.2 millimetres long.

- Yet the giant agrippa moth can have a wingspan of 30 centimetres.

- The heaviest insect is the Goliath beetle (below) from Africa. It is as heavy as two hen's eggs (100 grams).

Ninety per cent of all animals on Earth are insects. Our world is covered with these tiny **arthropods**. All arthropods have their skeletons on the outside of their bodies, like a case.

Insects are everywhere apart from in the oceans. Some live in deserts at over 40 °C, while some insect eggs can survive freezing. Insects have lived on our planet for 400 million years.

We know of about 1 million different species of insect. But there could be ten times that number.

So, what are insects?

Insects are air-breathing **invertebrates**, although some young take up **oxygen** from water Each adult has three parts to its body:
- the head and **antennae**, also called feelers
- the **thorax**, with three pairs of legs and often two pairs of wings
- the **abdomen**, with the heart and lungs inside.

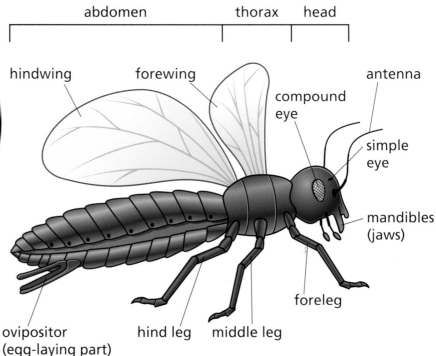

abdomen — thorax — head

hindwing · forewing · antenna · compound eye · simple eye · mandibles (jaws) · foreleg · ovipositor (egg-laying part) · hind leg · middle leg

Wild words   **abdomen** part of the body containing the stomach
arthropod animal with jointed legs, but no backbone

Many types

Some people think that any creepy-crawly is an insect. That is not true. Spiders have eight legs and are called **arachnids**. Woodlice have fourteen legs and are called **crustaceans**. Centipedes and millipedes have lots of legs! They are called myriapods.

It can be useful to put the main types of insects into eight groups. There are many other types of insects too, but this list helps you to see the variety.

Description	Number of species	Examples
Hard wings	400,000	beetles, ladybirds, fireflies, weevils
Scaly wings	150,000	butterflies and moths
Membrane wings	130,000	ants, bees, wasps, termites
Flies	120,000	flies, midges, mosquitoes
Bugs	88,000	aphids, water bugs, cockroaches, earwigs
'Fliers'	36,000	dragonflies, mayflies, damselflies, thrips
'Hoppers'	25,000	crickets, locusts (shown below), stick insects
Bristletails	370	silverfish

Find out later...

How do some insects attack others?

How do some insects avoid getting eaten?

Which insects do we need to fear?

invertebrate   animal without a backbone
thorax   part of the body between the head and abdomen, like our chest

Meet the family

How do all the the groups of insects differ from each other?

Incredible beetles

- The longest living insect is the jewel beetle. The **larvae** can live in trees for over 35 years before becoming adults. The adults have a far shorter lifespan.

- Did you know you might have eaten beetles? A female Mexican beetle is crushed to make a red dye and food colouring called cochineal. It is sometimes used in lipstick or in pink icing for cakes.

Hard wings

A quarter of all animals on the planet are beetles. For every person there are about 25 million beetles. Some are too small to see, while others are as big as your fist. They all have biting mouthparts and two pairs of wings. The front wings are hard wing covers that are not used for flying.

Of the 360,000 different species of beetle, perhaps the ladybird is most people's favourite. It may be because of its colour and spots. But gardeners like ladybirds because they eat greenfly, which would otherwise damage plants.

Other beetles are not so popular. About 40,000 species are weevils. These insects have long snouts like a trunk and they can destroy cotton crops, food and plants.

▶ These cochineal beetles live on a cactus.

antennae   insect's feelers
larvae   young of an animal that are very different from the adults

Scaly wings

Butterflies and moths belong to the second-largest family of insects. They have large wings that are **scaly** and powdery. These **species** go through an amazing change as they mature from the caterpillar stage to the adult.

What is the difference between a butterfly and a moth? Most moths fly at night and butterflies fly during the day. However, some moths break the rules and fly in daylight, like the clearwings moth. Some people think butterflies are brightly coloured and moths are duller. This is not always the case. There are dull butterflies and there are brightly coloured moths.

The best way to tell the difference is to look at their **antennae.** Butterflies generally have antennae with small lumps on the end, but moths do not.

Bright butterflies

Many new species of beetle and moth are found each year. There are about six times as many species of moth as there are species of butterfly. Butterflies and many moths have brightly coloured scales on their wings. The purpose of these patterns is to attract a mate.

▲ A ladybird opens its spotted wing cases to reveal its flying wings.

▲ This close-up of a butterfly's wing shows its powdery scales.

scaly   covered in scales, like a mosaic

Termites

Termites are often called 'white ants' because many are white. They live in large underground nests just like ants. Some nests have tall 'chimneys' above ground, like the one below. There are about 2250 different **species** of termite.

Ants, bees and wasps

Some insects always seem busy. They live in large groups and have to work hard to keep their nests clean, their young looked after and their queen fed.

Ants live in **colonies** made up of several classes. These include the winged ants and soldiers and the workers. Workers often carry things. An ant can lift 50 times its own weight. But that is nothing compared with the honeybee, which can lift 300 times its own weight. That is like a person lifting a full bus!

All bees, wasps and ants have a special skill. They can return to their nest after travelling long distances. They seem to have built-in **navigation**. When they find food, they have ways to tell the others where the food is.

colony   group of individuals living together
navigation   working out the right way to get somewhere

Busy bees

Most bumble bees live on their own in burrows or in tree stumps. Some live as far north as the Arctic. Bees are different from wasps because they feed their **larvae** with honey. They make this by collecting **nectar** from plants. Wasps feed their larvae on meat, usually insects that they **paralyse** with their stings.

Good workers

Bees have been important to us for centuries. They produce honey and wax and they help to **pollinate** plants. They do a huge amount of useful work every year.

Ants and wasps help to keep down the numbers of many pests on our crops. They eat caterpillars that harm cereals, vegetables and fruit. Scientists believe that if these families of insects were to disappear from the Earth, our way of life would fall apart.

Overcrowded

The largest recorded single colony of insects was a group of ants in Japan. There were over 300 million ants living in one super-colony of 45 joined up nests.

▼ These wood ants are coming out of their nest in the spring.

◄ Honeybee workers store **pollen** and honey in their nest.

---

paralyse   stun a creature so it is unable to move
pollinate   transfer pollen to the female parts of a flower to make seeds

Mosquito

The average mosquito has 47 teeth, but it is the mosquito's sharp **proboscis** that causes the trouble. It stabs through our skin to drink blood, which will make us itch.

The female *Anopheles* mosquito can pass a deadly **parasite** into the bloodstream. This spreads the disease malaria. Malaria kills millions of people every year. This makes mosquitoes the deadliest insect known to humans.

▶ A mosquito bites through human skin.

Flies

Flies are all over the world – billions of them. They have troubled us for hundreds of years. The common housefly has followed humankind to every corner of the earth. As it buzzes around a kitchen, a housefly settles on any food it can find. It may have just fed on a rotting rat or on animal droppings. Then it crawls over your pizza. Or it may lay eggs on food we leave uncovered. Maybe that is why we hate flies so much.

The mouthparts of flies can only suck; they cannot chew. They suck up liquids and spit them out again – which spreads disease.

FAST FACTS
- Not all flies can fly. Some fungus gnats, for instance, have given up their wings.
- A housefly always hums in the key of F.

parasite   animal or plant that lives in or on another living thing
pincer   hook at the front of some animals' mouths for holding food

Bugs

We often call any creepy-crawly a 'bug' but a true bug is an insect with a beak-like mouth for piercing and sucking. There are about 11,000 species of bug in North America, 5600 in Australia and 1600 in the UK. They vary in length from just 1 millimetre to 11 centimetres. The largest bugs include earwigs and cockroaches.

The longest of the 1200 species of earwig is from the island of St Helena in the South Atlantic. It can reach 8 centimetres but it is now feared to be **extinct**. All earwigs have a narrow body, a pair of **pincers** and a claw-like tail.

There are nearly 4000 species of cockroach in the world, but fewer than 1 per cent of them are pests.

Cockroach facts

- The largest known cockroach in the world has a wingspan of up to 18 centimetres.

- The smallest known cockroach is about 4 millimetres long and lives in the nests of leaf-cutter ants in North America.

- Australian burrowing cockroaches, like those shown above, can weigh the same as a hen's egg.

◄ A housefly on your food can spread all sorts of disease.

'Fliers'

Whether they run, hop or fly, adult insects know how to move fast. They have to escape from hungry mouths. Those that fly come in many shapes and sizes.

One of the largest is the dragonfly. **Fossils** have been found of dragonflies with a wingspan of 75 centimetres from 350 million years ago.

Today, dragonflies are fairly common near water in warmer parts of the world. There are about 5300 **species** worldwide, and these can be divided into two main types: the true dragonflies, that rest with their wings out from their body in a cross shape, and damselflies, that hold their wings parallel to their bodies.

Locusts

Sometimes desert locusts **swarm**. This is when up to 500,000 million locusts meet up. There could be 1 million tonnes of locusts flying in the sky, like a huge thundercloud stretching as far as the eye can see. They eat any plants they find. Such a swarm can eat 20,000 tonnes of grain in one day. That is enough to feed 20 million people!

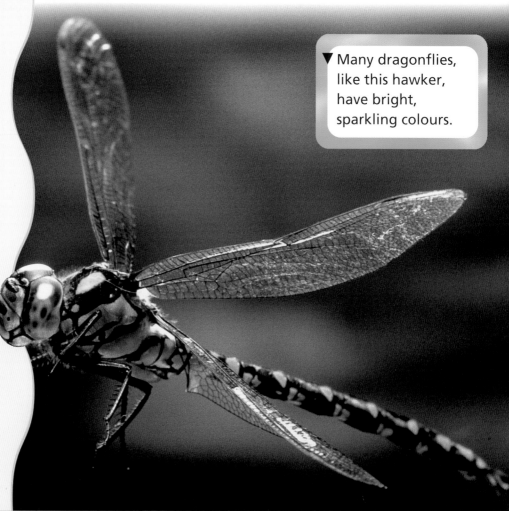

▼ Many dragonflies, like this hawker, have bright, sparkling colours.

fossil   very old remains of things that once lived, found in mud and rock

Springtails

Springtails are tiny insects about 1 millimetre long. (The ones on the left here are magnified.) They do the soil good by breaking down dead plant matter. Some are pests to crops. There are over 6000 species around the world. Scientists have found there can be 100 million springtails per square metre in the ordinary farm soil of Iowa, USA.

'Hoppers'

Fleas are hoppers and do not fly. They can jump 150 times their body length and 80 times their own height. Most are very small but the biggest flea in the world, which lives in North America, is about 12 millimetres long.

Grasshoppers have shorter **antennae** than crickets. They rub their back legs to 'sing', while crickets rub their front wings. Like locusts and grasshoppers, they hop and fly.

Slow movers

A praying mantis stands still with its front legs together as if it is praying. Stick insects do not need to move quickly because they spend their lives pretending to be twigs. But when a tasty insect comes by, they move fast to grab it. Stick and leaf insects live in the **tropics**.

FAST FACTS

- Thrips are less than 5 millimetres long. Swarms of these tiny flies often appear shortly before thunderstorms, so they are also known as 'thunder flies' or 'thunder bugs'.
- The longest stick insect can grow to be over 36 centimetres long – longer than this book.

Amazing bodies

Walking on water

Pond skaters like the one below can walk on water because they are so light. The **surface tension** on water stops them from sinking. Many waterproof hairs on their legs keep them afloat. They seem to skate over pond water with no trouble at all.

If they do not keep on the move, insects are likely to be eaten by **predators**. Their legs are important for running away from danger. But insect legs work in many different ways.

Legs

Cockroaches have three pairs of strong legs for running very fast. Grasshoppers use their back pair of stronger legs for jumping quickly.

Praying mantids use their front pair of legs like a weapon to catch **prey**. Dragonflies do not use their legs to walk but to catch other insects and hold them up to their mouths.

Butterflies use their legs to taste food as they have taste buds in them. Other insects use their legs for digging and swimming. Hairy legs are a great help to swimming insects. The hairs trap air and stop them from sinking.

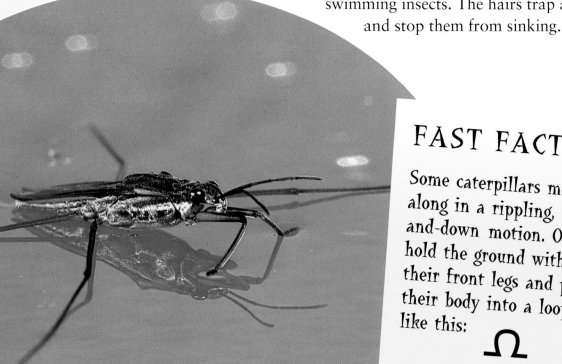

FAST FACTS

Some caterpillars move along in a rippling, up-and-down motion. Others hold the ground with their front legs and pull their body into a loop like this: Ω

predator   animal that hunts and eats other animals
surface tension   fine film across flat, calm liquid that can hold up light objects

Hopping legs

Fleas are famous for their power-packed legs that give them a huge flick into the air. With a strong breeze, they can travel a long way. From a sitting position, a flea can easily hop a distance of 30 centimetres. That is like a person doing a long jump of 140 metres. A flea was once recorded jumping over a metre high. That is like a person hopping over the Empire State Building!

Running legs

Silverfish are small wingless insects that spend most of their life under stones or floorboards. They are extremely fast – the only time you might see one is if it gets trapped in the bathtub. They can wriggle in and out of tiny spaces, such as between the pages of a closed book.

▶ This is a **time-lapse photograph** of a flea jumping.

Human head lice

Some insects do not move if they do not want to. Human head lice cling on to hair with a claw and they are impossible to remove even when hair is washed and combed. Even using conditioner that makes hair smooth and slippery cannot remove lice. Only special shampoo can get rid of them – or having your head shaved.

▲ This magnified view of a head louse shows it clinging to a hair.

As light as air

Many insects are so light that they can drift about in the air without much effort. Thrips and aphids are so small they can be blown by the wind for long distances. Other light insects can land and walk on ceilings. Sticky pads on their feet keep them from falling, and **gravity** has little effect when you are so light. Even if an insect falls, it will not get hurt when it drops on the ground.

Wings

Insect wings are full of tiny veins filled with blood. Butterfly wings are often covered in very small hairs. These trap air and help them flutter. Brightly coloured wings allow males and females to recognize each other.

Fast fliers

Dragonflies like the one above are some of the fastest insect fliers. They can fly in bursts of over 48 kilometres (30 miles) per hour. They often attack other insects in mid-air. Some migrate long distances.

Hawk moths are thought to be one of the fastest insects and have been measured flying at 53.6 kilometres (33.3 miles) per hour.

► These **time-lapse photographs** show a fly taking off.

gravity   force that pulls all objects to the Earth
migrate   travel in search of food or to breed

Did you know?

- Ladybirds were sent into space in 1999. Even in zero-gravity the ladybirds could fly well and hunt aphids.

- A hover fly is brilliant at flying. One minute it can dart so fast that it is just a blur and then it can hover and seem to hang in the air, like the one below.

Flying

Most insects have two pairs of wings, but some are wingless, such as lice, fleas and silverfish. Many flies only have one pair of wings. Most bugs and beetles do not use their front wings for flying but to protect their flying wings and their bodies.

A lot of insects are ace pilots. They can perform amazing stunts, from landing upside down on a ceiling to hovering over a flower. Butterflies and moths can flutter gently as well as do **vertical** takeoffs and fly backwards. Some fly incredible distances. North American monarch butterflies travel more than 2400 kilometres (1500 miles) south to Mexico every winter. Other species **migrate** even further and cross the Arctic Circle. The flying skills of many insects are truly amazing.

vertical   going straight up in the air

Seeing colours

For many insects, flowers are food. Whilst feeding, bees and butterflies collect **pollen** grains and transfer them as they feed on other flowers. This **fertilizes** the flowers so they can produce seeds. To help insects see them, many flowers have striking colours with bright markings. These attract and guide the insects.

Heads and senses

The insect brain may be tiny but it has a lot to do. It is the control centre that must respond to all the signals picked up by the insect's senses. Each insect needs to know where three things are: danger, food and a mate.

Eyes

Most insects have two **compound** eyes, made up of any number of single eyes. They help the insect to see moving objects clearly and to work out distances. Dragonflies, with their flying skills, need good eyesight, so their compound eyes are bigger than most other insects' eyes. Simple eyes just tell an insect where it is light or dark. Insects that live under ground or in darkness may have no eyes at all.

▼ Bright colours are a big draw for a bee.

compound   made up of many parts
fertilize   when sperm joins an egg to form a new individual

Signals

Insects use sounds to help them make sense of their surroundings. They also pick up **vibrations** with their **antennae**.

Grasshoppers and locusts have ears on their **abdomen**. These help pick up sounds of their own **species** so they do not become separated. The lacewing picks up sound vibrations with its wings, while ants do so with their legs.

Crickets spend a lot of time chirping to each other. But their ears might not be where you would expect them to be. Crickets have their ears in their front legs.

Hairy legs are important for cockroaches, too. Tiny bristles sense sound vibrations and warn them if a heavy foot is about to stamp.

Night flight

Lights often attract insects at night. This can be harmful to them if they are attracted to a flame. Experts think one reason why moths fly into a light is because they depend on stars and the moon to find their way, and artificial light upsets their **navigation**.

◀ The compound eyes of an emperor dragonfly are seen clearly here.

> ▶ A male gypsy moth has an amazing sense of smell.

Finding the right place

Lice use their antennae to sense the warm damp parts of our bodies that provide a good feed. Hair lice are not too fussy what sort of hair they choose, although they often like to lay their eggs in clean hair.

> ▼ Under the microscope, this head louse on a hair looks like an alien monster.

Antennae

Antennae poke out from an insect's head like two aerials that pick up signals in the air. They are often called 'feelers' because they are used to touch and feel **vibrations**.

Antennae can often also sense chemical changes around them. Most insects communicate using smell but they do not have noses. Instead, they have small **sensors** over their bodies, but especially on their antennae.

Many moths have antennae that look like small feathers. These can sense other moths over long distances. A male gypsy moth can smell a female more than 1.6 kilometres (1 mile) away.

A cockroach uses its long antennae to feel its way in the dark. That is how it tracks down crumbs at night as it scuttles about the kitchen.

abdomen   part of the body containing the stomach

Picking up signals

Antennae come in a wide range of shapes, sizes and lengths. Each antenna is divided into **segments**. Scientists can sometimes tell from these segments if two insect species are closely related.

Insects that live together in close groups often stroke and groom each other with their antennae. Honeybees use theirs to communicate messages.

A bee will sometimes fly into the hive and dance. It waggles its **abdomen** and moves in a figure of eight. The other bees crowd around and touch the dancing bee with their antennae. This tells the other bees in which direction and how far to fly to find the flowers.

Heat sensors

Blood-sucking insects use their antennae to sense the heat from **warm-blooded** animals. Mosquitoes and botflies can feel temperature changes and then fly in for a drink of blood. For some reason, it seems that mosquitoes are particularly attracted to people who have just eaten bananas!

▼ A mosquito's feathery antennae can be seen in this magnified photograph.

Finding air

- Mosquito **larvae** hatch in water but they have to get oxygen from the air. They breathe through tiny tubes that they poke out of the water.

- Diving beetles like the one below collect bubbles of air at the surface and carry these bubbles under water with them as a source of oxygen.

Breathing

All animals need to take **oxygen** into their bodies. Their blood takes the oxygen to the muscles, organs and brain. These let out **carbon dioxide**, which the body has to get rid of. Land animals do this by breathing with lungs while fish breathe with **gills**. The gills are slits near the head, which take oxygen from water flowing through them.

Most insects breathe through tiny tubes inside their body called tracheae. Air enters the tubes through holes in the sides of the body. Insects such as water beetles and water boatmen still breathe like this and regularly have to rise to the surface to take in fresh air. However, their **larvae** do not have to worry – they are born with gills.

> > > > > > > > > >
Find out more about larvae on page 34.

carbon dioxide   gas that animals breathe out
oxygen   one of the gases in air and water that all living things need

Strange bodies

The larvae of dragonflies, damselflies, stoneflies and mayflies breathe through gills. They hatch out in water where some grow and develop for up to five years before they climb out. Then they shed their skin and fly off as adults that breathe through tracheae.

Insect blood is rich in **nutrients,** but not as rich in oxygen as our blood. It is not red, either, but usually a watery green. The insect heart is a tube which runs along its back. It beats to swish the blood around the body. This keeps the important oxygen flowing to all the organs and muscles.

Insect blood does not flow through blood vessels (tubes) as ours does. It flows through spaces inside the insect's body.

▲ An elephant cannot get rid of its lice by having a shower.

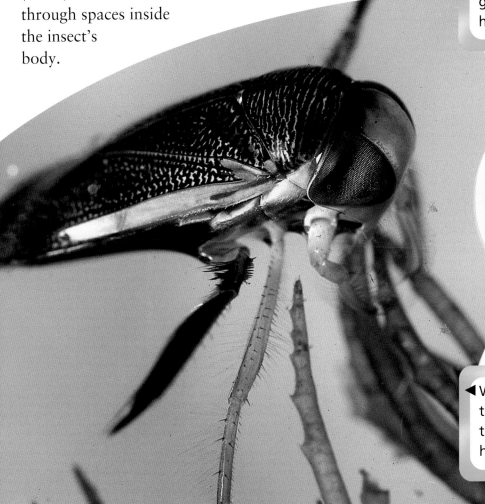

Breathing under water

Even though lice do not have gills, they will not drown if their **host** goes for a swim. Tiny air bubbles trapped in skin **pores** or hair will give lice enough oxygen to **survive.**

◄ Water boatmen row themselves through the water, using their hairy legs as oars.

pores   tiny holes in the skin
tracheae   tubes that air passes through

Feeding

Tear moths

A moth from South-east Asia gets a drink in the strangest of ways. It feeds on the water in the eyes of cows. It settles under their eyes and drinks their tears. These tear moths do not seem to upset the cows – at least, they are nothing to cry about!

The mouths of insects vary according to what they eat. Some, like hawk moths, have tongues up to 15 centimetres long. These are for probing deep into flowers to find nectar. The male mosquito also feeds on plant juices. But the female mosquito's **proboscis** has a needle point to break skin and drink blood.

Some ants can bite through tough skin, including a human's. Their jaws are strong so they can grip and cut up other insects.

Flies can only suck liquids. When they land on solid food, they spit juices on to it from their spongy mouth pad. This **dissolves** the food into a soupy mess, which the fly can then suck up and enjoy.

▶ The jaws of a leaf-cutter ant are like saws.

crop　pouch in the throat for storing food
dissolve　break down into a liquid

Digestion

Once food gets into an insect's mouth, it begins to break down. **Saliva** and other juices along the digestive system work on the food so that it is ready to go through the gut. Here, it is absorbed into the insect's blood. The nutrients are then taken to the cells of its body.

Many insects have a **crop** below their mouths. This is a storage pouch, which lets the insect gulp down food quickly. The crop can then empty over time as the food passes into a **gizzard**. This is very useful for animals that do not have teeth in their mouths. The gizzard is like a second mouth that grinds up solid bits of food before they pass into the stomach. Any waste passes through the insect and is finally pushed out.

Thirsty beetle

Even in dry deserts, some beetles manage to get moisture. The darkling beetle of Africa's Namib Desert (shown below) points its **abdomen** into the sea mist. Tiny droplets of water collect on its body, which it then licks.

gizzard   extra stomach that grinds down food
saliva   juices made in the mouth to help chewing and digestion

Jumping beans

Caterpillars from a Mexican moth hatch inside a bean that grows on a plant. They feed on the seeds inside the bean (shown below). When the bean falls to the ground, the caterpillar inside moves about suddenly. This makes the bean hop about. Children in Mexico hold races with these 'jumping beans'.

Plant-eaters

Over half of all insect species are **herbivores**. That means they only eat plants. These might be leaves, stalks, roots, pollen, **nectar**, seeds, fruit, bark or wood. Any gardener will know of the many insects or **larvae** that can infest and destroy plants. Farmers spend a fortune on **insecticides** to stop their crops being ruined. Not all attacks are as dramatic as the locust **swarms** that can strip a field in minutes. Most tiny insects are unseen as they chew, suck or bore into plants. It is our fault there are so many insects in the world. Farming on such a large scale has let insect numbers grow. Without humans providing so much food, there would be fewer insects in the world.

FAST FACTS

Millions of insects are eaten by wild animals such as fish and birds every day. If these animals disappear, insect numbers will grow out of control.

fertilizer   nutrients for the soil to feed plants
herbivore   vegetarian or plant-eater

Insect gardeners

The leaf-cutter ant does not eat leaves but cuts them up for **compost**. It takes them to its nest to feed to a special type of **fungus** that it grows for food. The fungus gardens are deep inside the ants' nest. As leaves reach the nest, they are cut up and licked clean of anything that may harm the growth of the harvest fungus. Next, the ants spread out the leaf bits mixed with their droppings. This acts as **fertilizer**. As the fungus grows, it is fed to the members of the **colony**.

Many termites feed on wood, which is hard to **digest**. The termites have help from tiny animals that live inside their guts. They are called protozoa and they help the termites break down the wood fibres.

Plants that bite back

Some plants get their own back on nibbling insects. The Venus fly trap (shown above) waits for a fly to land on it before its leaves snap shut and trap the insect inside. The sundew traps insects on its sticky hairs. These plants slowly digest the stuck insects.

◄ These leaf-cutter ants are carrying leaf pieces that they will use to make compost.

insecticide   poison to kill insects
protozoa   very tiny living things that can only be seen with a microscope

Scavengers

A number of flies, such as the flesh fly and the bluebottle shown below, lay their eggs in rotting flesh. **Carrion** beetles also home in on a dead animal and begin chewing. Such insects are the undertakers of the animal world and help to keep the **environment** clean.

Predators

Many insects kill. One third of all insects are either **predators** or **parasites**. Tiger beetles, wasps and ants are active hunters. They spend a lot of time looking for prey. Other insects lie in wait for prey to come to them. A praying mantis keeps very still and when **prey** comes close, it thrusts out its legs to catch it. The mantis bites the neck of its prey to **paralyse** it and then begins to eat. The mantis almost always starts eating the insect while it is still alive. This makes sure that the insect's struggle is soon over and it does not attract other predators. A praying mantis eats beetles, butterflies, spiders, crickets, and even small tree frogs, lizards, mice, hummingbirds… or another passing mantis.

▼ A praying mantis waits to strike.

carrion   dead and rotting flesh

Parasites

Insects need to lay their eggs close to food. **Larvae** must eat when they hatch. To make sure the food is fresh and warm, some flies lay their eggs inside a living animal. Their maggots hatch and feed on live meat.

Warble flies lay eggs on cattle and their larvae burrow into the cow's skin. They feed inside the cow's flesh until they are ready to fly away.

The sheep nostril fly also lays eggs on a live **host**. The eggs hatch in a sheep's nose and burrow into its eyes and brain. Other flies depend on the host licking eggs and getting them into its stomach. Many horses swallow botfly larvae, which then grow in the horse's **intestines**. Most pass out in the horse's droppings but some burrow into its blood vessels.

Eaten alive

Some flies lay their eggs on spiders. The larvae hatch and eat their way through the spider's body. Some wasps inject their eggs into caterpillars. The eggs hatch out and slowly eat the caterpillar alive – from the inside.

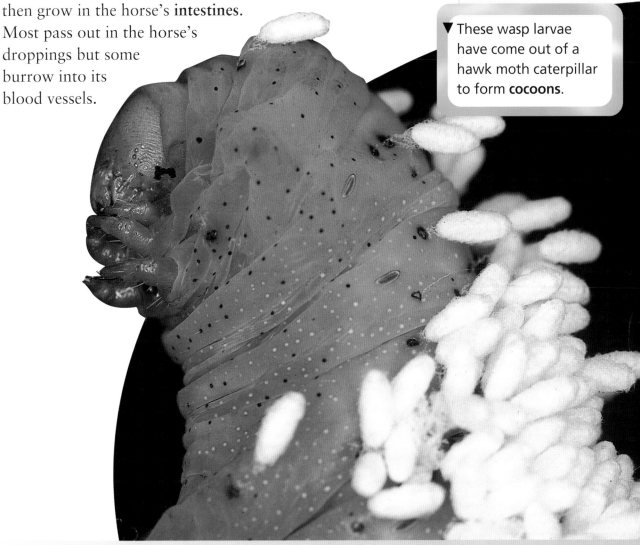

▼ These wasp larvae have come out of a hawk moth caterpillar to form **cocoons**.

Revolting meals

Some insects have the most revolting of tastes. Their mouths water at the sight of blood, rotting flesh or dung. The fouler the smell, the faster they arrive.

Lice

Sucking lice feed on fresh warm blood and they only live on mammals. That can include humans. A female louse will lay about 300 eggs at the rate of about 10 eggs a day. The eggs take 5–10 days to hatch. The **larvae** will not leave in a hurry, even if the **host** happens to die. Lice can **survive** for up to three days on a dead body. Then they hitch a ride on a passing fly to be taken to a new host.

Blood

Although fleas can live for a few months without food, they cannot survive or lay eggs without blood. Adult fleas that have just come out of their **cocoon** can only live about one week if they cannot get a blood meal. The flea above is feeding on a mouse.

▶ Dung beetles roll a dung ball back home. They are among the strongest insects and can lift 50 times their own weight.

cocoon   silky case that protects larvae

Dung

Flies like to lay eggs in dung. A cowpat can hatch out 2000 flies. In Australia there are around 20 million cows dropping twelve cowpats each a day. That means a lot of flies!

Luckily, dung beetles eat dung. They gather fresh dung into balls to roll into underground nests. The female lays an egg into each dung-ball and covers the nest with soil. Without these beetles, the world would be piled with dung.

Cows were only brought into Australia in 1788, so the dung beetles there were only used to kangaroo dung. They would not eat wet, smelly cow dung. Dung beetles from Europe and Africa had to be brought in to deal with the cowpats and cut down on the number of flies.

17 June 2003
Live beetles appear in boy's urine

A thirteen-year-old boy in India has amazed doctors. Live winged beetles appeared in his **urine**. He said: "No one believed me when I told them about these flies." A doctor treating him at Bengal hospital said, "This is a very rare condition called myiasis, in which a human or animal body, dead or alive, is invaded by the larvae of particular flies."

◀ Maggots like these were once used in hospitals to clean wounds. They ate dead flesh, which helped the wound to heal.

Breeding

Gift-wrapped

Before they mate, male dance flies give their partners a present of a dead insect wrapped in silk. The female is so busy unwrapping this that the male can mate with her without being eaten. Sometimes he fools her by wrapping up nothing – which is a mean trick.

An insect's life is usually short. Finding a mate and making more insects become urgent jobs.

Meeting

Insects have many ways of finding and attracting partners. Their **antennae** are tuned in to seek out a partner. The female is often busy giving off chemicals to help the male find her. Sometimes the male sings for her, or he will dance using his antennae and wings. As soon as they meet, the insects often rub antennae or legs.

Male fireflies are a bit flashy. They attract a mate by glowing in the dark. The males have light organs under their **abdomens**. The dancing greenish-yellow to reddish-orange lights impress the wingless female. Sometimes, after **mating**, her eggs will even start to glow.

▲ Dance flies go through a complex courtship before they mate.

mate   when a male and female animal come together to produce young

Mating

Male insects are often smaller than the females. This can be dangerous if the female is used to eating smaller insects. The male has to transfer **sperm** into her body without being eaten by her. Often the male will be sick to give the female something to eat. It may not be romantic but it saves his life.

The female stores his sperm inside her body until she releases her eggs to be **fertilized**. She finds somewhere safe with food close by to lay the eggs. Some insects, such as aphids and tsetse flies, give birth to live young. Many water bugs carry their eggs on their backs and look after their young once they have hatched. Female earwigs like to keep things tidy by licking their eggs clean.

▲ This wood wasp is laying her eggs into beetle larvae under the bark.

Wood wasps

The **larvae** of some wasps and beetles grow hidden under tree bark. But a female wood wasp can sense these larvae under the bark. She injects her eggs through the bark and right into a larva. When the wood wasp eggs hatch out, the grubs feed on and kill their poor young **host**.

◄ A firefly looking for a partner gives off a warm glow!

sperm   male sex cell

Strange timing

Cicadas are large bugs that make a chirping sound. There are about 1500 species around the world and their nymphs live in soil. In North America, some cicada nymphs take 17 years to shed their skins and become adults. Millions of adults emerge at the same time.

Young and parents

Insect eggs hatch into either tiny wriggling grubs called **larvae** or into small adults, called **nymphs**. The nymphs of dragonflies, cockroaches and grasshoppers do not have wings, only small wing buds. Most nymphs shed their skin as their bodies get bigger.

The female mayfly lives under water for up to three years as a nymph. When she becomes an adult and grows her full wings, she has about a day to mate and lay her eggs. She cannot eat or drink and will die within the day.

Many young insects go through major changes to become adults. This is called **metamorphosis**. A larva will eat for a few weeks, shed its skin and then become a **pupa**. Many insects go through these four stages: egg, larva, pupa and adult.

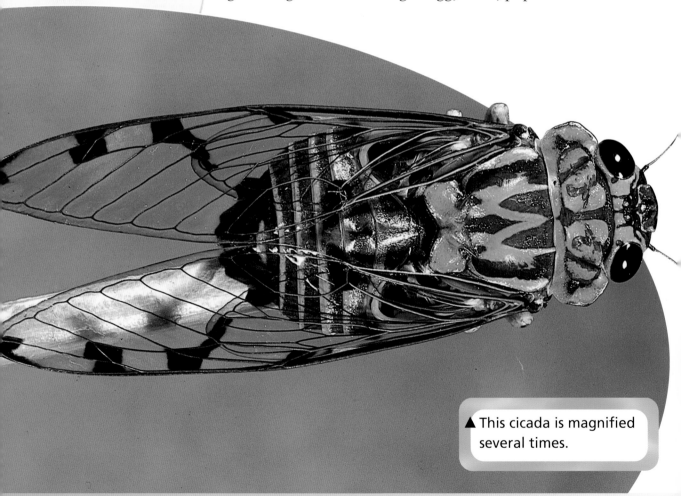

▲ This cicada is magnified several times.

metamorphosis   change from being a larva to being an adult

Young mantids

Female mantids, such as the praying mantis, lay groups of 12 to 400 eggs in a frothy liquid. This hardens into a shell where the tiny insects survive during the winter. There are about 1800 species of mantid and some even **survive** winters in the north-east USA. They were brought to the USA to keep down the populations of other insects.

Tiny mantid nymphs **emerge** in the spring. Their first meal is often one of their brothers or sisters. The nymphs look like ants at first then grow during the summer as they eat aphids (greenfly) and flies. Finally they shed their last skin and emerge as fully grown adults.

▶ Mantid nymphs look like small versions of the adults.

Did you know?

Leafhoppers and froghoppers are small bugs that suck sap from plant stems. As nymphs, they wrap themselves in bubbly froth to protect them from the sun and from **predators**. These bubbles are often called 'cuckoo spit', shown above.

STOP PRESS

A Cambridge University professor has discovered that froghoppers are the kings of the jumping world. They can leap similar distances to fleas, despite being 60 times heavier.

nymph   in-between stage from larva to adult
pupa   stage when a larva is developing into an adult inside a shell or cocoon

Life cycle

It is amazing how a crawling caterpillar can change into a fluttering butterfly or moth. It completely changes in shape and colours – and it suddenly knows how to fly.

The female monarch butterfly lays about 400 eggs under the leaves of milkweed plants. The yellow eggs take about two weeks to hatch. The new caterpillar is only 2 millimetres long, but it eats straight away. On the first day of its life, it eats its own weight in food. The tiny caterpillars begin to strip the milkweed leaves as they munch through the plant.

Do not touch

The caterpillars of the monarch butterfly (shown below) are brightly coloured and stripy. This is a warning to **predators** that they taste horrible and should be left alone. The caterpillars eat milkweed leaves that make them poisonous.

When it reaches 5 centimetres, a caterpillar begins to change into a **pupa**. It weaves a small silk button under a leaf, sticks to it, and waits.

chrysalis   pupa of a butterfly or moth, with a hard outer case
cocoon   silky case that protects larvae

New life

Inside its casing, the pupa is slowly changing shape and colour. The outer layer hardens into a green case, with gold dots. This is known as the **chrysalis**, which is the Greek word for 'golden'. Inside this chrysalis, strange things are happening. A butterfly is slowly forming.

When the butterfly starts to **emerge** two weeks later, its wings are droopy and wet. It clings to the old chrysalis case while **fluid** from its **abdomen** is pumped into the veins of the wings. After a few hours the wings are dry with no creases. The butterfly is now ready to fly away. All it has to do next is find a mate, and the process starts again.

On the move

Each autumn thousands of monarch butterflies gather in southern Canada before **migrating** south to Mexico. But many of the trees in Mexico that have been homes to these butterflies for years are being cut down. Monarch butterfly numbers are now falling.

◀ This monarch butterfly has just emerged from its chrysalis.

fluid   liquid that flows easily

Defence

Insects face danger all the time. Running away is one defence but sometimes other tricks help them **survive**.

A prickly customer

Camouflage is a great defence. Treehopper bugs from Florida, USA look like thorns, as seen below. Even if a predator does risk taking a bite, the treehopper's shape makes it stick in most throats.

Colour and camouflage

Looks can be a matter of life and death. An insect will soon be someone's dinner if it is easily seen. Insects that chew leaves all day are easy targets for **predators**. Leaf-eating insects have **evolved** many ways to survive attack. For instance, many **species** feed only at night, when there are fewer birds about. Insects often hide by feeding on the undersides of leaves. Beetles drop off a plant as soon as they sense a predator is near.

camouflage   colour that matches the background
disguise   change of appearance to look different

How to stay safe

Some insects are experts at staying hidden. Moths with **mottled** brown wings can stay safely on tree trunks, and a bark bug looks just like a tiny bump on a tree. It is difficult to spot stick insects and leaf insects when they sit on a branch. Many insects have just the right colouring to blend into their background so they stay unseen.

Disguise is always a good trick. A flower mantis looks like a flower when it sits on a bush. Some grasshoppers stay very still in mud or on rocks and look just like pebbles.

Keep off

Many moths have two large spots on their wings, which look like staring eyes on a scary face. The swallowtail caterpillar (shown above) has a good trick. It has two large eye-spots on its back so it looks like a poisonous snake.

◄ The pupa of a swallowtail butterfly looks like bird droppings, but it turns into a beautiful butterly.

evolve   develop and change over time
mottled   spots and patches of colour

Clever tricks

Leaf-feeding insects have a hard time. They are near the bottom of the **food chain**, as many other animals want to eat them. These insects have to come up with a few extra tricks to defend themselves. Many do not try to hide at all. Their bright colours seem to say, 'Come and get me.' Yet all **predators** know one thing – when an insect is brightly coloured, it could mean that it is poisonous. Many colourful insects feed on leaves that make them **toxic**. Their colours simply warn others to keep away. But sometimes harmless insects copy them. Despite being really good to eat, they are covered in bright spots and stripes.

▲ A bright buckeye butterfly warns, 'Keep off'.

Colourful tricks

Birds know to leave monarch butterflies alone. The bright orange of the butterfly warns all predators that they are poisonous because of the plants they eat. Even butterflies that are not toxic may copy the monarch butterfly and show bright warning colours – just to be on the safe side.

food chain   order in which one living thing feeds on another
gland   part of the body that makes hormones and other substances

Fighting back

One way to scare off attackers is to hit back. Even if a predator is much bigger than you, giving it a shock can give you time to scurry or wriggle away.

The caterpillar of the puss moth puffs up its head if it is under threat. It pokes out a pair of horns and if that fails, it squirts acid from just under its head. This stings any attacker and makes it think twice.

A wood ant also puts up a fight with a secret weapon. It will lie on its back and poke out its **abdomen**, then squirt acid. It runs off while the attacker's eyes water.

The giant weta is from New Zealand. When under threat, it just kicks out with its strong back legs – covered in spines.

Smelly tricks

Another way to avoid being eaten is to smell. The stink bug (shown below) has **glands** near its back legs. When under threat they ooze a liquid with a disgusting smell. Many stink bugs are brightly coloured as an extra warning.

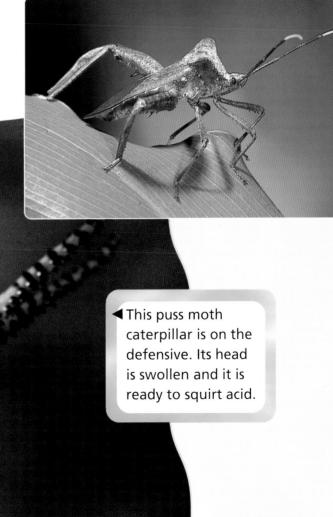

◄ This puss moth caterpillar is on the defensive. Its head is swollen and it is ready to squirt acid.

toxic   poisonous

Scary insects

Some insects have a bad reputation. Many people tremble at the thought of them.

Cockroaches

Everyone seems to hate the cockroach. We think of them swarming in filthy dark places, spreading disease. However, many **species** of cockroach are small and live in very clean places.

Cockroaches are **scavengers** and they feed on almost anything. Many just eat wood but a few give all cockroaches a bad name. They spread disease when they go from dirty areas into kitchens. They can **contaminate** food so they need to be controlled.

Cockroaches are tough so it can be difficult to control them. They have been around for millions of years. They can even **survive** doses of **radiation**. Water does not bother them, either. They can survive for 40 minutes without air, so they do not often drown.

Enough to make you shudder

One reason cockroaches are scary is because they can be hard to kill. After all, a cockroach can live for a week without its head. It will only die because it cannot drink water and dries out. A cockroach can survive without food for up to a month.

▼ The giant burrowing cockroach may look scary, but the only thing it is likely to bite is dead leaves in forests in Australia.

contaminate   spoil and make unsafe
radiation   rays of energy that can be harmful in large amounts

Unwelcome visitors

Most species of cockroach live in the tropics but some can survive at the North and South poles. Yet most cockroaches cannot deal with temperatures much colder than freezing, so they often like to move indoors. They can easily climb walls because they have claws on their feet. In the days of wooden sailing ships, cockroaches were carried all over the world. They were the **stowaways** of the insect world.

People hate the thought of cockroaches coming from the sewers into their homes. It can be horrible to find them in your kitchen or bathroom as they scuttle about at night.

Did you know?

'Ghost cockroaches' like the one below are often seen at night. A cockroach that has just shed its skin is white with black eyes. After about eight hours the shell returns to its normal colour.

◄ There are more than 3000 species of cockroach. Only 60 species are pests, like these German cockroaches.

scavenger   animal that feeds off scraps and the prey of others
stowaway   someone who hides on a ship to get a free journey

On the move

Killer bees first escaped from Brazil in 1957. Swarming killer bees may attack someone 40 metres away and chase them for up to 400 metres. Strong smells, bright colours and loud noises send them wild. The only advice is to keep running.

FAST FACTS

For a normal, healthy person to get a deadly dose of bee venom, it would take about twenty stings for each kilogram of body weight. That is about 1500 stings at once for a 70-kilogram person.

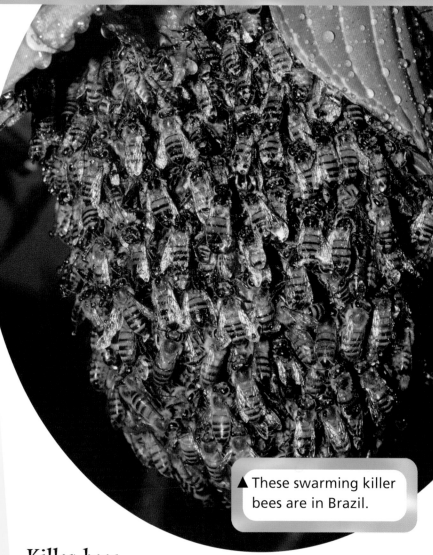

▲ These swarming killer bees are in Brazil.

Killer bees

Killer bees sound like insects from a horror film. But there is a type of bee in Africa that is much more **aggressive** than the normal honeybee. If many of them **swarm** and attack someone, they can be dangerous.

Maybe another bee is scarier. Fifty years ago, Brazilian scientists tried to breed a new bee to produce more honey. But they created a bee that turned nasty very quickly. Some escaped and began to spread. They flew north from Brazil and were first seen in the USA in 1990. These new bees will swarm and attack at loud noises. Even jumping into water will not keep them away – they just wait for you to come back up for air.

aggressive   hostile, angry and likely to attack

Scientists in Texas are working hard to stop the advance of killer bees. They have set traps and are concentrating on queen bees. If they can **fertilize** killer queen bees with **sperm** from ordinary honeybees, they hope to stop more killer bees hatching.

28 March 2002

Killer Bees Attack Woman in Las Vegas

A swarm of killer bees attacked a 77-year-old woman in Las Vegas. 'She had over 500 stings on her arms, chest, face and head,' a city spokesman said. The woman was in a critical condition at University Medical Centre after she was rescued by the Fire Department.

Dangerous stings

Some people have an **allergy** which means they can die from bee stings. It is thought that more people die from bee stings each year than from the bites of poisonous snakes. Even so, fewer than 1 per cent of people have a severe reaction to bee stings.

▲ A honeybee's sting and **venom** sac are at the end of the **abdomen**.

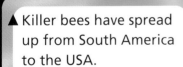
▲ Killer bees have spread up from South America to the USA.

Marching teeth

Army ants kill and eat most animals that do not get out of the way. Together they can kill lizards, snakes, chickens, pigs, goats, scorpions and many other animals. They also climb trees and eat birds or insects that may live in trees. They have even been known to eat people asleep in their beds.

Scary ants

What animal will eat any other animal in its path, raid ant **colonies** and march miles to find food? The army ant.

Army ant colonies have one queen and many thousands of workers and soldiers. They travel around together and set up camps. The ants join together to protect the queen and her eggs. They fasten on to each other using their jaws and tiny claws. Their jaws are particularly strong and sharp.

A report told of army ants **swarming** over an area 1.6 kilometres (1 mile) long, moving across Brazil in 1973. According to some news stories, the chief of police was too slow to get out of their way and was eaten alive. It took a real army with flame-throwers to force the ants to march back into the forest.

▶ Army ants swarm over a forest floor in Trinidad.

swarm   move together in a large group

Fire ants

Another ant from South America can be scary. Red fire ants inject **venom** that burns and blisters the skin. The venom begins to break down cells and **tissues** and can make someone feel quite ill. These ants are now common in parts of the USA.

Red fire ants reached Alabama in the 1930s on cargo ships. Colonies soon began to spread. The first time people knew about them was in 1942. Ed Wilson, a thirteen-year-old boy, came across a mound on the land next to his home. Scientists were amazed to see them, and also to find that each colony had more than one queen. This is seen only with the North American red fire ant. Within 30 years, these ants had swept across the southern United States.

Stinging ants

The bulldog ant of Australia, like the one below, has strong jaws. It bites without letting go and injects strong venom. As few as 30 stings from an ant like this can kill a human.

tissue   soft parts of the body – collections of cells

Insects in danger

Looks can kill

In parts of Europe, the hornet (shown below) is under threat due to its bad image. People kill them because they look harmful, but they rarely attack humans. Now people are trying to protect them in southern England and their numbers are starting to rise. They have also been introduced to Canada and the USA.

With so many **species** of insect in the world, we are not always aware of those in danger of being lost forever. Being so small and often out of sight, many insects will not be missed until it is too late. People care less about insects than larger animals because we do not see most of them and those that we do see are often pests.

For many years we have been at war with insects. We have soaked much of our planet with **insecticides**. We destroy their nests and **habitats**. People catch butterflies, moths and beetles to display in glass cases. A number of species are now **endangered**.

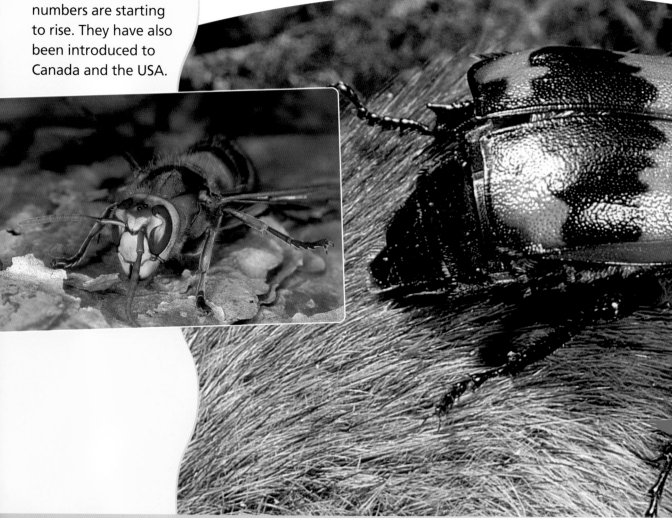

endangered　at risk of disappearing forever
habitat　natural home of an animal

Three victims

There is an insect that lives in an 11-kilometre (7-mile) stretch of sand dunes in Utah, USA. It has a long name but it is only 1 centimetre long. It is called the coral pink sand dune tiger beetle. There are about 1000 left. Collectors take them because of their shiny colours and stunning appearance. Off-road vehicles also disturb their habitat.

The American burying beetle has orange and black stripes and it is the largest **carrion** beetle in North America. This beetle is on the endangered list because there are fewer animals for it to eat. Boston University has released some of these beetles into the wild in Massachusetts, USA.

The basking malachite is a shiny green damselfly about 4.5 centimetres long. There are now only about 1000 left in South Africa because cattle have destroyed the riverbanks where they breed.

Making a comeback

Although it is called the large blue butterfly, it only has a wingspan of 2 centimetres. Clearing hillsides for farming and the use of weed killers and **insecticides** wiped out this butterfly from Britain in 1979. It was re-introduced in 1983 and since then a small number have bred in the wild.

◄ This burying beetle is feeding on the body of a dead animal.

insecticide   chemical sprayed to poison insects

Insects help police

A dead body soon starts to rot. Insects eat it or lay their eggs inside the **tissues**. Scientists have found that different insects arrive in a particular order. This can help them work out the time of death of a murder victim.

Insects and us

We often think of insects as things to be squashed rather than as animals of value. Yet without insects our planet would starve.

Many insects are very useful to us. They help keep the Earth clean, they help plants make fruit seeds, and they feed millions of animals.

Yet we still shudder at the thought of fleas, lice and cockroaches in our homes. Termites eat wood and cause great damage to houses. Pests like the Colorado beetle attack potato crops in many parts of the world and cause great suffering. Locusts wipe out crops and cause **famine**.

▼ Colorado beetles like these can destroy tomato and pepper plants as well as potatoes.

famine   long period of poor crops, no harvest and no food

Curse and blessing

You are never far from an insect. Most of the time, we are unaware of them – until they bite or sting us or spread disease to our animals and us. In 1350, fleas on black rats spread a disease called bubonic plague, killing one-third of all Europeans.

Yet the insect world is finely balanced. If we use poisons to destroy one insect pest, this will have an impact on many other **species**. Many insects are a great help to the soil and to plants. Insects are vital to the world's **food chains**. Insects keep our planet alive.

FAST FACTS

A bat can eat as many as 600 mosquito-sized insects in one hour. An average-sized bat colony may eat 500,000 insects in one night.

A deadly curse

The *Anopheles* mosquito is the most deadly animal on the planet. It carries the disease malaria, which in the last 2000 years may have caused half of all human deaths. It still kills between 2 million and 4 million people each year.

Bill Gates, the world's richest man (shown above), has given US $168 million to help scientists find a cure for this deadly disease.

Find out more

Websites

Enchanted Learning
The 'Coloring Pages' have pictures, activities and information on insects.
enchantedlearning. com

Bugbios
The 'Entophiles' pages have fantastic photos of insects.
insects.org

BBC Nature
Website with quiz and information on insects.
bbc.co.uk/nature/ animals/wildbritain/ look_around/insects

Books
Animal Groups: Life in a Colony of Ants, Louise and Richard Spilsbury (Heinemann Library, 2003)
Animals of the Rainforest: Ants, Christy Steele (Raintree, 2003)
Animals of the Rainforest: Butterflies, Eric Braun and Sandra Donovan (Raintree, 2003)
Bugs and Insects Spotters' Guide, A. Wooton (Usborne, 2000)
Classfying Insects, Andrew Solway (Heineman Library, 2003)

World Wide Web
If you want to find out more about insects, you can search the Internet using keywords like this:
- 'insect flight'
- swallowtail + caterpillar
- stick insect

You can also find your own keywords by using headings or words from this book. Use the search tips below to help you find the most useful websites.

Search tips

There are billions of pages on the Internet so it can be difficult to find exactly what you are looking for.

For example, if you just type in 'water' on a search engine like Google, you will get a list of 50 million web pages! These search skills will help you find useful websites more quickly:

- Use simple keywords instead of whole sentences
- Use two to six keywords in a search, putting the most important words first
- Be precise – only use names of people, places or things
- If you want to find words that go together, put quote marks around them
- Use the advanced section of your search engine
- Use the + sign between keywords to link them. For example, typing + KS3 after your keyword will help you find web pages at the right level.

Where to search

Search engine

A search engine looks through millions of websites and lists all sites that match the words in the search box. It can give thousands of links, but the best matches are at the top of the list, on the first page.
Try bbc.co.uk/search

Search directory

A search directory is like a library of websites that have been sorted by a person instead of a computer. You can search by keyword or subject and browse through the different sites like you look through books on a library shelf.
A good example is yahooligans.com

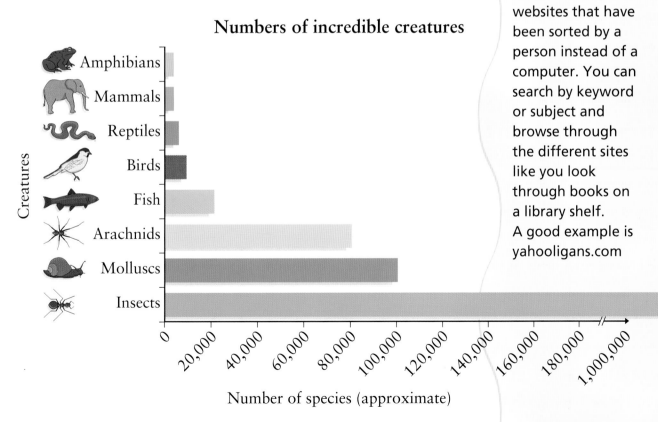

Numbers of incredible creatures

Creatures (vertical axis): Amphibians, Mammals, Reptiles, Birds, Fish, Arachnids, Molluscs, Insects

Number of species (approximate): 0, 20,000, 40,000, 60,000, 80,000, 100,000, 120,000, 140,000, 160,000, 180,000, 1,000,000

Glossary

abdomen part of the body containing the stomach

aggressive hostile, angry and likely to attack

allergy nasty reaction to certain substances

antenna (plural: **antennae**) insect's feeler

arachnid arthropods with eight legs, including spiders and scorpions

arthropod animal with jointed legs, but no backbone

camouflage colour that matches the background

carbon dioxide gas that animals breathe out

carrion dead and rotting flesh

chrysalis ('kris-a-lis') pupa of a butterfly or moth, with a hard outer case

cocoon silky case that protects larvae

colony group of individuals living together

compost manure or rotting plants used to enrich the soil

compound made up of many parts

contaminate spoil and make unsafe

crop pouch in the throat for storing food

crustacean ('krust-ay-shun') arthropods with a hard shell, including crabs and lobsters

digest break down food in the body

disguise change of appearance to look different

dissolve break down into a liquid

emerge come out into view

endangered at risk of disappearing forever

environment natural surroundings or habitat

evolve develop and change over time

extinct died out, never to return

famine long period of poor crops, no harvest and no food

fertilize when sperm joins an egg to form a new individual

fertilizer nutrients for the soil to feed plants

fluid liquid that flows easily

food chain order in which one living thing feeds on another

fossil very old remains of things that once lived, found in mud and rock

fungus type of mould that grows in damp places

gills organs that some animals have to breathe under water

gizzard extra stomach that grinds down food

gland part of the body that makes hormones and other substances

gravity force that pulls all objects towards the Earth

habitat natural home of an animal

herbivore animal that has only eats plants

host animal or plant that has a parasite living in or on it

insecticide chemical sprayed to poison insects

intestines end part of the digestive system after the stomach

invertebrate animal without a backbone

larva (plural: **larvae**) young of an animal, that is very different from the adult

mate when a male and female animal come together to produce young

metamorphosis change from being a larva to being an adult

migrate travel in search of food or to breed

mottled spots and patches of colour

navigation working out the right way to get somewhere

nectar sugary liquid made by plants

nutrient important substance found in food and needed by the body

nymph in-between stage from larva to adult

oxygen one of the gases in air and water that all living things need

paralyse stun a creature so it is unable to move

parasite animal or plant that lives in or on another living thing

pincer hook at the front of some animals' mouths for holding food

pollen a flower's male sex cells, which combine with female cells to make seeds

pollinate transfer pollen to the female parts of a flower to make seeds

pores tiny holes in the skin

predator animal that hunts and eats other animals

prey animal that is killed and eaten by other animals

proboscis long mouthparts of some insects, like a trunk

pupa stage when a larva is developing into an adult inside a shell or cocoon

radiation rays of energy that can be harmful in large amounts

saliva juices made in the mouth to help chewing and digestion

scaly covered in scales, like a mosaic

scavenger animal that feeds off scraps and the prey of others

segment section or separate part

sensor device that picks up signals

species type of animal or plant

sperm male sex cell

stowaway someone who hides on a ship or plane to get a free journey

surface tension fine film across flat, calm liquid that can hold up light objects

survive stay alive despite danger and difficulties

swarm move together in a large group

thorax part of the body between the head and abdomen, like our chest

time-lapse photograph photo that shows the stages of an action that happens quickly

tissue soft parts of the body – collections of cells

toxic poisonous

tropics parts of the world where it is warm all year round

urine waste liquid that is passed out of the body

venom poison

vertical going straight up in the air

vibration quivering movement or fast trembling

warm-blooded able to keep the body warm even if the outside temperature is cold

Index

Series in the *Freestyle Curriculum Strand* include:

Turbulent Planet

Energy Essentials

Incredible Creatures

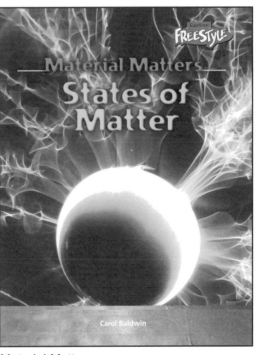

Material Matters

Find out about the other titles in these series on our website www.raintreepublishers.co.uk